Flower ARRANGING

A QUANTUM BOOK

Published by
Chartwell Books
A Division of Book Sales, Inc.
114 Northfield Avenue
Edison, New Jersey, 08837
USA

ISBN 0-7858-0677-6

This book was produced by
Quantum Books Ltd
6 Blundell Street
London N7 9BH

Produced in Australia by Griffin Colour

Flower
ARRANGING

Rona Coleman

CHARTWELL
BOOKS, INC.

HOLDING AND
FIXING FLOWERS

A successful flower arrangement depends on how firmly it is anchored to the base. There are several methods of preparing containers and bases; floral foam is now so much a part of the flower arranger's basic equipment that it is difficult to remember how we ever made an arrangement without it. But, efficient though it is, it is certainly not the only way of supporting the material; in fact, some flowers prefer to be directly in water whenever possible. Proteas, in particular, last far longer if they can stand in deep water, while gladioli, although they last quite well when arranged in foam, really prefer to have their stems in water.

Wire mesh, pinholders, moss, sand and cut branches all help to support the material and your choice of method must be dictated by the size and type of design, as well as the material being used.

Many arrangers like to use mesh as well as foam. This is a very valid method, particularly for rather large heavy material. Mesh used alone should be crumpled to fit the shape of the container, preferably with some left well above the rim. If you press it in too low, you will have no support for your lateral stems. Even though it may seem fairly firm, it is advisable to secure it to the rim of the container with adhesive tape or string.

If you are using a container with an extremely high glaze, or made of glass, the

An old-fashioned wire support in a wide-mouthed urn. Both support and urn pose problems: the urn requires a very large number of flowers for a balanced design, and the wire support (superseded by more modern floral foam and mesh) is very difficult to handle. Definitely a container to leave well alone.

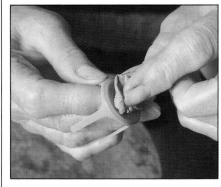

Soaked floral foam will need to be secured to a shallow 'open' base. (*Above and top*: It can be impaled on prongs which have been attached to a plastic saucer by Oasis-fix. Both prongs and container must be clean and dry if the Oasis-fix is to adhere firmly.

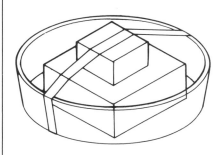

A foam base should stand at least 1 in (2 cm) above the rim of your container. Deep bowls may need two pieces of foam stacked to achieve sufficient height. A second smaller piece may be impaled on the first and the two secured firmly to the container with adhesive tape.

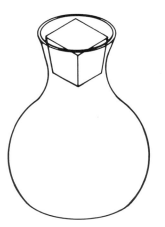

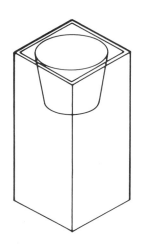

It is important to cut soaked foam to a size that will fit securely into the neck of your container. A square piece should be wedged into a round neck and a round piece into a square neck. This ensures a good fit and leaves room for adding more water when necessary.

A large pot of this kind (*right*) and also in the diagram (*far right*) can be made smaller by inserting a smaller pot into its neck. This solves the problem of securing the foam sufficiently well to carry a big design. It also reduces the amount of water — and therefore of additional weight — needed to keep the flowers and foliage fresh.

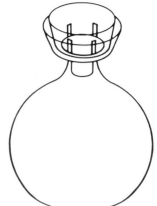

In large containers with narrow necks, candle cups may be inserted to reduce the size, but even the largest cup may be unable to carry sufficient foam for a big design.

Mesh is particularly useful as extra support for heavy designs. It should be fixed to your container with a loop of adhesive tape secured on either side. With a large container, the mesh may need to be secured in three places.

Oasis-fix will not adhere firmly enough. The solution is to fold a piece of tissue or paper kitchen towel and use it as a small non-skid mat for the foam. The block should then be fixed firmly with sello-tape.

Sand is sometimes used at the base of a container for dried flowers. But be very careful, for sand is heavy and if too much is used, it could make the base of the vase fall out.

If you are totally without any support mechanism, cut some stems or small branches to the depth of the vase. Almost fill the aperture and they will give the necessary support, though a design with spreading lateral lines would not be practical.

In deciding the size of foam, the main thing to remember is that once you have inserted a stem you have made a hole which obviously weakens the block. If you have never used foam, cut a piece you feel will take every stem comfortably. If your container has a round opening, then choose a square piece of foam, and vice versa. This allows for a better fit and there will be a space left to insert the spout of the watering can for adding more water.

The depth of the foam is easier to estimate. Since most arrangements have some lateral stems, make sure the foam stands at last 1 in (2 cm) above the rim of the container otherwise you will be trying to insert stems into mid-air.

Pinholders of varying sizes are useful for shallow containers. They are very heavy and need no fixative to hold them in position. They can also be used together with wire mesh for larger arrangements that include heavy branches and flowers with large stems, for example, arum lilies. They will also tolerate foam, but much prefer to be directly in water.

Large containers, of course, present a greater challenge than smaller ones. For example, the type of brass container sometimes used in churches becomes impossibly heavy if filled with water, while the neck is often rather small. One solution to the problem is to locate a smaller container that will effectively slot into the neck thus forming a kind of inner lining. Alternatively, a large candle-cup may be used, though even the largest size may not be big enough to hold a piece of foam large enough to support a really large design.

Each time you make an arrangement, try to keep the size of foam used down to a minimum. Although it is far easier to design into a large block, it needs a lot of material to mask it which is, at least, time-consuming. But never make it so small as to risk the foam collapsing. Like many other skills, there are certain guidelines to follow, but eventually, one becomes experienced in what your tools – in this case, the foam – can do for you.

Remember, before you begin a design, to add water to the container as soon as you are satisfied that the base is firm. It is far easier at this stage than when all the material is in place.

In order to travel with a design, it is safer to pour the water out when the arrangement is finished, and take a small can with you to refill the container once it is in place. The well-soaked foam will keep the flowers fresh for many hours but in a warm atmosphere you will get a longer vase life from the flowers if the container is kept filled with water.

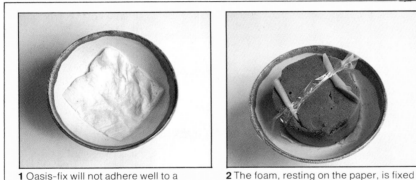

1 Oasis-fix will not adhere well to a highly-glazed surface. A damp tissue placed in the base of this shallow compote will stop floral foam from sliding.

2 The foam, resting on the paper, is fixed with sellotape. The two pieces of stem seen here will prevent the tape from biting into the foam.

3 Here soaked foam has been laid on a polystyrene tray to protect the surface of the silver container. The foam is firmly secured to the tray with sellotape.

4 For display purposes, a damaged leaf can be patched on the underside with a section from another leaf. Use a little glue, plus a little care, to complete the disguise.

For this contemporary free-style
arrangement (*left*) a large pinholder is
sufficiently heavy to sit firmly in the shallow
highly-glazed dish. The decorative stones
help to mask the pinholder so that the
minimum of foliage is needed. Each stem
should be held very close to the pinholder
and impaled firmly (*above*).

THE FOUR BASIC FORMS

Each of the four basic forms described here provides a simple geometric structure on which a flower arrangement can be built. The materials you have at hand and where you decide to place your arrangement, will determine the form you choose to work from.

The history of flower arranging dates back to ancient times and all kinds of patterns and forms have evolved through the ages, mainly under the influence of the West and the Far East. The Japanese, for example, have practised the art for well over a thousand years, and they are renowned for their pure classic asymmetrical designs. Books, paintings and mosaics are a valuable historic record – there are the Byzantine floral mosaics in Ravenna with their tall symmetrical designs, the stylized Dutch and Flemish flower paintings of the seventeenth and eighteenth centuries, and the proliferation of books and magazines on the art of flower arranging in Victorian times. Definite rules of arrangement, however, were established during this century.

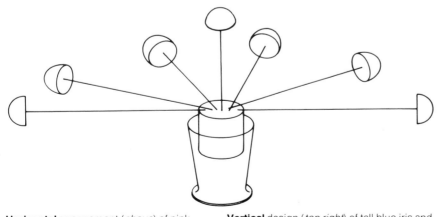

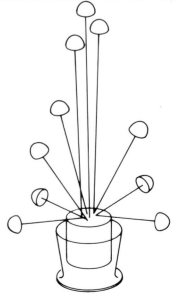

Horizontal arrangement (*above*) of pink carnations, pink bud tulips and gypsophila. One more tulip is needed on the left to complete the symmetrical form.

Vertical design (*top right*) of tall blue iris and yellow double gerbera. To keep their upright form, the gerberas are supported with an inner wire.

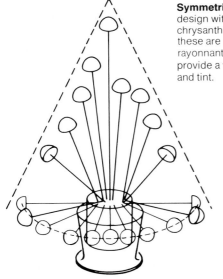

Symmetrical five-point design with spray chrysanthemums. Some of these are the spidery or rayonnante type, which provide a variation in form and tint.

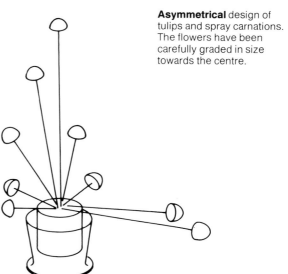

Asymmetrical design of tulips and spray carnations. The flowers have been carefully graded in size towards the centre.

HORIZONTAL ARRANGEMENTS

Arrangements with a horizontal emphasis are particularly suitable for table centrepieces where the design should not be so high and bushy that it acts as a hedge between the diners. It is also an excellent style for 'window-dressing' an empty fireplace in summer, or a mantelshelf, particularly in a fairly small room where a tall design might otherwise be overpowering.

While too many rigid rules and regulations applied to what is not only a technical skill but also an art form, can be stultifying to progress, some of the most obvious rules do make sense. For example, most basket shapes would suggest a horizontal arrangement and that the handle should be left free from encompassing foliage so that it is easy to hold. On the other hand, there may be instances where the designer might feel it necessary to place a few tall flowers above the handle. However, in order to break the rules, one must first learn to apply them. To avoid frustration and disappointment, it is better to stick to basics until you feel your designing is becoming more fluid.

Sometimes a flower arranger is invited to place flowers on the church altar, though in some churches this is not

A subtle horizontal design from Korea, composed of pink dahlias, yellow roses and white antirrhinums enlivened with variegated foliage.

allowed. A horizontal design is usually the most suitable and should be kept symmetrical to balance the existing symmetry, and often the simplicity, of other appointments nearby. Having completed the design, always go to the back of the church to check that the central flower is not taller than the cross, which is either on or just behind the altar. It is usual when making a horizontal arrangement to establish the spread of the design first. Fix these two lines first and then decide the height and the depth and work within this framework.

Arrangements for the dining table whether at home or at a banquet are

Carnations, with a frosting of gypsophila. The tulips were added last to give variation of colour, shape and texture.

usually horizontal otherwise no one would be able to see or be seen. The maximum width of such designs is crucial, for there must be ample space for the guests to eat or, in the case of a banquet, speakers' notes and microphones. Graceful and near-symmetrical horizontal designs, sometimes joined with ribbons or ropes of green foliage can effectively enhance what might otherwise be a rather stark dining table. This is one of the many occasions that offers both scope and challenge to any designing enthusiast.

1 To make a horizontal design, first decide on the colour and texture of your design and gather your materials together. Here the yellow and orange of the flowers pick up the colouring of the foliage at the centre.
2 Cut well-soaked floral foam so that it fits the container you have chosen.
3 Not every design need be constructed from the outside inwards. Begin in the middle of this design, masking the foam with foliage and roughly describing the shape intended.
4 Now insert your line flowers.
5 Strengthen the lines with the addition of more flowers, being careful not to overcrowd the arrangement.

VERTICAL ARRANGEMENTS

A simple description of vertical is that the line is at right angles to the horizon. If one then translates horizon into container-rim, it will give a good idea of how material should be set in place. However, most things turn out better if a plan of action is followed and a flower arrangement ought, in effect, to begin with a plan, based on a logical framework.

First establish whether the arrangement is to be a facing design – that is, viewed from the front only – or an all-round design. This affects the position of the first main stem. For a facing design, the main line must be set in towards the back of the foam, and for an all-round arrangement, it should be set in the centre of the foam.

The main line should be straight and definitive, and establish the maximum height of the arrangement. Then, two or three more lines should be inserted very close to the first one and parallel to it, each one slightly shorter than the previous one. These will emphasize the main line and help to make it visually stronger.

The next decision is to determine the maximum width of the design. For a facing arrangement, insert two lateral stems aiming towards the position where the main line was inserted.

For an all-round design, insert five stems of equal length radiating from the central line.

All that remains to be done is to add further material at intervals, keeping within your established framework. Take care not to crowd the material – it is always better to have too little rather than too much.

Strong vertical arrangements of purple irises softened by downward curving stems of yellow forsythia (*right*) and a charming combination of freesias with chrysanthemums (*far right*). Notice the interesting positions of the flower heads and the way in which profile and full views combine to make a flowering composition.

Straight-stemmed flowers like the gerbera (*above*) are particularly suited to vertical designs. The gerbera may curve, but wiring will ensure that the flower remains upright.

1 To wire a flower, insert a piece of wire of the correct thickness downwards through the centre of the flower stem into the middle of the flower head.

2 Press the wire gently but firmly back into the centre of the flower with the blade of your knife. Care is needed to ensure the flower remains undamaged.

SYMMETRICAL ARRANGEMENTS

This is the purest form of all design. Perfect symmetry or visual balance is present in classical architecture, sculpture, tapestries, medieval paintings and containers, yet few of us are consciously aware of it. Even the word itself suggests grace and elegance.

The technical definition however, is far more mundane meaning that the object should be divided into two parts, both being equal in content. Translated into terms of flower arranging, this does not mean that all designs have to be facing. They can be circular, oval, horizontal or vertical, as long as they can be equally divided. Thus, a design with vertical emphasis may also be symmetrical, or the reverse, for it might quite possibly be asymmetrical and still be vertical.

As few flowers are identical, it is not easy to achieve perfect symmetry with living material. Therefore, an arranger is not expected to measure the two sections exactly for height, width and depth. Your design should rather appear to be symmetrical, giving a satisfying visual balance, bearing in mind, of course, that the basic disciplines should be respected. If your lines are well-placed and the materials carefully chosen, then successful results should follow. A simple arrangement can be made by placing an even number of stems at either side of the central stem.

In choosing the material it is probably easier to get a satisfactory result if you use not more than three types of flower, that is, flowers of differing shapes and sizes, such as delphiniums, roses and spray chrysanthemums. Apart from the type of flower and colour, the classic 'recipe' includes *line* flowers, which are the materials that give gradation, normally with buds and semi-open flowers, plus materials for *emphasis*. These are usually mature blooms, often of a strong, clear colour and shape.

Strong, clear lines are first established (*inset*) for this beautiful symmetrical arrangement of yellow double freesias, darker yellow spray chrysanthemums and purple liatris, with interesting dark green foliage, to emphasize the yellow blooms.

Your choice of colour will naturally play an important role in determining symmetry. You may, in fact, make a design which is entirely symmetrical from the point of view of line, yet if the colour values are off-balance, it will never appear to be symmetrical. Do not let this deter you from making symmetrical arrangements for table centrepieces and display. The style cannot possibly be mastered in one easy lesson, so keep trying out different types of materials during each season of the year. Remember that it is better to begin with a simple design and graduate to more complicated ones as you gain confidence.

For this arrangement the base is first masked with green hellebore (*above*) before the three main lines are set in place (*below*).

Notice (*right*) how the third flower down to the right of centre has been placed so as to avoid too formal an effect.

ASYMMETRICAL ARRANGEMENTS

This form of design is the reverse of the symmetrical type – which is, that each side should be different, possibly in content and certainly from the point of view of line and emphasis.

However, as with the other forms, it needs a firm framework on which to build. So, although the main line may not necessarily be set into the middle of the arrangement, it must be seen to be the main line that runs straight into the centre of the design.

Asymmetrical arrangements can also be set vertically or horizontally, but care should be taken so that they are not confused with free-style designs.

However, try not to become intimidated by too many definitions, rules and regulations. These few pointers are intended to help and not to confuse. When you are making an arrangement, imagine, in essence, that the framework is made up of bare twigs which you will then 'dress' with flowers and foliage. Keep the basic structure simple and well-defined to ensure a successful arrangement.

White jug and flowers in the first stages of preparation (*above*). Foam is wedged into the neck and the main lines are set in place. Notice the small but very definite bud carnations describing the structure.

At the next stage (*above*), existing lines are strengthened with more flowers, and some foliage is inserted. The main lines are now to some extent masked.

Vertical emphasis. Tulips and spray carnations in an elegant vase.

Pink carnations alone would be rather bland, so a little red alstroemeria is added. Notice

how the main structure is kept, while at the same time flowers and foliage is added.

A strong structure described with lemon antirrhinums (*left*), which is repeated at varying lengths. Brown spray chrysanthemums at the heart of the design provide variation in colour and form.
Above: A mixed arrangement of freesia, spiced with a few stems of tolmiea and strengthened at the heart with alchemilla foliage.

BALANCE AND PROPORTION

In flower arranging both balance and proportion, like colour values, are largely a matter for the individual eye. However, one cannot escape the fact that *actual* balance is needed for the design to be stable. It will either balance or fall over – it is as simple as that. It may seem impossible for arrangements to collapse and overbalance, but they do, with very disappointing results. Fortunately there are several technical ways of preventing this.

It may clarify the situation to pinpoint one or two problem areas. The first one is the size of the foam block. The size needed is most difficult to resolve since everyone works differently. But before cutting your foam, decide what kind of material you plan to use. If it includes heavy woody stems, or thick stemmed flowers such as gladioli and delphiniums for example, or heavy blooms such as chrysanthemums and dahlias, then you will need a fairly large and deep piece of foam. It should be remembered that every time a stem is driven into a block of foam, it makes a hole exactly the size of the stem. So, if you begin without a clear plan and have to change the position of the stems many times, the block is weakened still further.

In most cases, you may use only one or two chunky stems with quite delicate flowers such as spray carnations, candytuft and other lightweight annuals, or even spray chrysanthemums.

In deciding the depth of the foam, you will soon see, with a little experience, when a deeper block is required. For instance, a horizontal arrangement will need more than a vertical design.

When all the foregoing points have been sorted out in your own mind, and really, it only takes a moment or two, your next step is to make absolutely sure that the foam block is going to remain firm in its seating. Where practical, use an Oasisprong plus adhesive tape wrapped around at least twice. When it comes to tackling the design, it is a good idea, if you are not too sure of your plan, to 'sketch' the lines out on the table with some of the

1 To make a two-tier arrangement First, choose two basketware trays. Loop strong wire off-centre through the larger, bottom one and twist this over a soaked foam block, using small pieces of foliage to protect the edges.

2 Pull the two ends of wire up through the top tray, which will now rest on the foam below, held in place by the wire. Flatten the wire ends.

3 Take a small tin lid and attach it to the top basket tray with Oasis-fix, again off-centre, and fill it with a piece of soaked floral foam.

4 Begin the design by placing the four stems of allium. Insert one stem laterally into the bottom foam block and the others into the top tier block.

5 Insert the foliage into the foam on each level and add the carnation stems and the remaining green material.

6 The completed design (*opposite*), fully exploiting the quality of the allium.

An unimaginative use of four allium (*above*). They clearly want a little support material, and the stark stems need some back up. Adding deep red spray carnations and foliage in a design on two levels makes a far more interesting and dramatic use of the allium.

material. Or, you could even work into an old piece of foam as a practice run.

The pedestal is probably the type of design that gives the most difficulty where balance is concerned. But at the risk of being repetitive, begin by placing your material right at the back of the foam. To make it safe, put your point of balance two-thirds towards the back of the foam inserting only a few stems into the front portion.

Visual balance is affected or influenced as much by the colour, size, shape and texture of the material, as the way in which it is used.

One of the best critics of any arrangement is a camera lens, for one's eye can see what one intends it to see, which is not always what is recorded by the camera. So, whenever possible, take pictures of your designs, aiming the lens exactly at the centre of the arrangement. It is not fair on yourself to shoot from either too high or too low for then the result will appear to be off-balance.

This pottery container (*above*) is too deep and too wide for such delicate flowers as sweet-scented freesias. The rough texture of the pot is also too heavy and tends to overpower the flowers.

Right: A solid-looking handmade pot is well suited to these large gerbera, arresting in shape, texture and colour. The pot was prepared with a good-sized block of soaked foam, wedged into its neck and further secured with adhesive tape.

Another way of checking your final design is to leave it, if possible, for 24 hours and then look at it as if seeing it for the first time when your judgement will be sharper.

Proportion should be seen in every aspect of the design, including the materials used, the proportion of the complete design in relation to the container, and the relationship of the chosen design with its environment.

While varying sizes of material can be used to create a good design, they should be selected with care so that they blend together. Thus, an arrangement of gerbera and freesia might be out of proportion. Even the *masking* and *support* foliage can sometimes upset good proportion. When using delicate flowers, such as freesias or Singapore orchids, the foliage should not be too large or heavy from the point of view of colour or texture. However, problems of bad proportion regarding the use of materials are, happily, few and far between. On the other hand, the choice of container is sometimes in error, for it may be too large or too small for the material. This fault is easily corrected by substituting another container.

A well-balanced arrangement of freesias in this chalice type vase (*above left*). But be warned — a wide-mouthed container like this demands many flowers if a satisfying design is to be achieved.

Above: This old-fashioned type of kitchen jar has become very popular and they can be used most successfully to complement modern interiors. The polyanthus are visually heavy enough here, but cowslips are too delicate.

Left: This handmade pot with its 'Celtic' pattern is an excellent choice for dried flowers. However, flower and design are both wrong here — the dried molucella is not only off-balance but too long for the vase.

TEXTURE AND CONTRAST

In flower arranging texture is as important as contrast. It is so easy to get carried away by including so many different textures in a design that in the end it lacks contrast.

In order to get the very best out of your materials, it is important to be aware not only of the individual character of flowers and foliage – their size, shape and colour values – but of their surface textures. Compare for instance, the texture of a rose with a carnation, a gazania with a chrysanthemum, or the shiny leaves of ivy with the dull fronds of grass. This will enable you to contrast rough with smooth, shiny with matt, plain with patterned and so on, to give a finer, more subtle dimension to your designs. It is worth looking out for this type of material and experimenting by contrasting texture with small and large, pointed with blunt or broad with narrow, to give an endless variety to all of your many designs.

Even within one flower there is variation in texture. The anemone-centred spray chrysanthemum, far right, has a knobby centre surrounded by a frill of smooth satiny petals. Like many other flowers, the passion flower, also, has its own built-in texture and contrast. The smooth outer circle of petals with a very fine fringed inner ring in purple, contrasts sharply with the cream.

The sameness of just carnations arranged in a round container as an all-round design (*top*) is spiced with gypsophila (*below*) — to give a softer, fuller effect with pleasing textural contrasts.

An interesting study in colour, line and texture (*right*). Notice how the rough weave of the container has been included in the design, and its low horizontal form balanced against the verticals and curves of the flowers.

All white flowers (*above*), each one different in texture size and shape, can become a challenging exercise. Two or three variations may give just the right balance to a design especially if it is complemented with suitable foliage. The permutations seem almost endless.

It is not easy to find a suitable container for these beautiful smooth anthurium flowers (*left*). Brass echoes the texture and shape and is visually heavy enough to underline the design.

PRINCIPLES OF
COLOUR SELECTION

It is said that if you want to create a positive impression on your business associates, then have a red wall in your office. It is maintained that this colour will act as a backup to the executive aura. In addition to having a specific total value, each colour is said to have a connotation related to human reaction. Thus red is positive and signifies power. Blue is the most introvert colour and implies faith and sometimes meekness, even timidity. Orange is supposed to suggest pride in the nicest sense of the word, while violet denotes gentleness and piety. Green indicates sympathy and compassion, while white is the very essence of light and signifies purity.

The first step is to clarify the primary colours: they are red, yellow and blue. All other colours are made from these in varying degrees of intensity. The primaries can be mixed to produce secondary colours, for example, blue and red make violet, yellow and blue make green, while yellow mixed with red produces orange. You may wonder what this has to do with flower arranging since we cannot stir a yellow daffodil and a scarlet tulip together in a bowl and produce an orange lily. In flower arrangement it is a question of understanding the values of each colour we use in order to produce the effect we want. For example, a vase with seven scarlet tulips and three pale blue irises would not be at all impressive or interesting, as red is an extrovert dominant colour while blue is receding and gentle. In short, the irises would be totally swamped by the red flowers.

Undoubtedly, colour has a definite effect on our senses, so it is worth remembering that bright, striking effects can be made by using warm colours, such as red, orange and warm yellows (these are the advancing colours), while more soothing and delicate designs can be made by using cooler blue-pinks, mauves, blue and purple (these are the receding colours). Grey foliage can also be used in cooler arrangements.

An arrangement with varying levels of one colour, such as pale pink through

to red, is described as being monochromatic. This category of colour harmony is usually very restful on the eye.

To choose any three neighbouring colours on the colour wheel, for example, from pink through red to mauve, will give you a harmonic colour scheme. In terms of flowers, this type of colour scheme is very pleasing indeed.

For a more striking effect, experi-

Lilac, liatris and berberis in a half-glazed Chinese ginger jar. Notice how the receding colour of the berberis emphasizes the flowers in this radiating design.

ment with complementary colour schemes. These are the colours that are directly opposite each other on the colour wheel, such as violet and yellow, blue and orange or green and scarlet. Do not necessarily choose the basic hue, but try to use

Too much of one type of material can be overwhelming. A vertical arrangement consisting of two varieties of lemon and yellow spray chrysanthemums needs another texture and colour to spice it up.

A 'cottage' arrangement (*above*) in a small mass-produced pottery pedestal. Red anemones, a little mauve honesty and a few brown spidery chrysanthemums are lifted from being too sombre by adding just a few bright yellow spray chrysanthemums.

Left: A contrast of texture is needed in this arrangement of spidery chrysanthemums, which looks slightly ragged and 'thin', without style or substance.

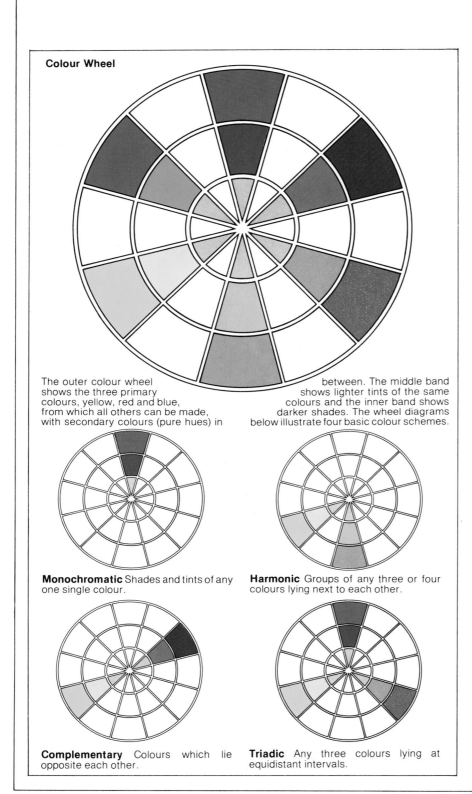

Colour Wheel

The outer colour wheel shows the three primary colours, yellow, red and blue, from which all others can be made, with secondary colours (pure hues) in between. The middle band shows lighter tints of the same colours and the inner band shows darker shades. The wheel diagrams below illustrate four basic colour schemes.

Monochromatic Shades and tints of any one single colour.

Harmonic Groups of any three or four colours lying next to each other.

Complementary Colours which lie opposite each other.

Triadic Any three colours lying at equidistant intervals.

tints and tones of each one. If you use them in well-balanced proportions you will produce very agreeable results.

One point to bear in mind with regard to colour in relation to living flowers is that their colours do change slightly every day. As the flower dehydrates, so the colour drains from it. Some flowers fade more noticeably than others, but in spite of their transient nature, we can enjoy them for as long as they have colour.

Lighting is very important in flower arranging – the colours of both flowers and foliage will look quite different if the arrangement is placed in a dark corner or on a window sill, or if it is seen under different types of electric light. Blue and mauve for instance, lose the crisp, clear colour that natural light gives them and become a rather dull grey under electric light. Fluorescent lighting, on the other hand, will enhance blue though it will make red appear a muddy brown. Tungsten lighting is appropriate for red, orange and yellow.

Daylight and electric light cast different shadows, so if you want your flowers to look their best under electric light, arrange them at a time when your choice of electric light is turned on.

The correct colour, form and texture will also give shape to a design. Colour perspective is built up by graduating and complementing the tonal value of each local colour. Light colours will stand out and become the focal point in your arrangement if you place material of a deeper tonal value behind them. Similarly you can use local colour that has lighter tones to soften and enhance colours that have darker tones.

The subtle use of local colour to create perspective in flower arranging is closely allied to techniques used by artists to give perspective to their paintings. Indeed, the artists of seventeenth- and eighteenth-century Dutch and Flemish flower paintings were instrumental in showing flower arrangers how emphasis and depth could be achieved in this way.

Here sharp colour contrasts emphasize the tonal value and details of the carnation.

Contrast between black and white is strong and makes the white flower stand out.

Similar tones of flower and background colours emphasize the yellow in the petals.

This green has a lighter tonal value than the second and creates a nearer image.

Here, the darker tone of green creates depth and the flower also recedes.

Green appears to emphasize the colour and contours of the carnation.

Detail and contrast are reduced because the tonal values are too similar.

The blue background recedes from the vibrant red carnation.

The yellow and red are both advancing colours with similar tonal values.

HARMONIZING
COLOURS

In flower arranging, harmony is almost as complex as it is in music. And 'that which forms a consistent or agreeable whole' must be our objective. We must not only use flowers and foliage that are in harmony from the point of view of colour, form and texture, but also in respect of the character of the material. Yes, flowers do have character; compare an arum lily with a violet; a daffodil with a rose.

The material must also harmonize with its container and its surroundings. For instance, a severe-line arrangement based in a wonderful silver dish intended as decoration for a brick fireplace in a sixteenth-century country cottage would not be in keeping with the background. A more simple style of design arranged in a copper or basketware container would be more in harmony with these rustic surroundings.

But always remember that in flower arranging, as in music, enjoyment of the end-product is the main aim, so do not be worried if your concept of harmony does not agree with other people's.

Magenta spray carnations (*above*) are an agreeable choice for the dull red of this rough-finish brick container, while sprays of honeysuckle blend the two colours together.

A charming old-world jug with a bouquet of anemones on the front (*below*) is the obvious container for these long-stemmed anemones. It is quite a luxury to find these flowers with such long stems, so the design was contrived to use as much of the stem and its natural curve as possible. These are arranged in a block of foam, which fits neatly into the neck of the jug.

This tall container (*above*) makes a lovely base for deep blue/mauve irises, pale mauve honesty flowers and pinky mauve freesias. The straight stems of the irises are set in symmetrically, while the honesty sprays provide a softer outline in contrast.

Left: Cerise spray chrysanthemums, pale pink spray carnations and alstroemeria almost exactly echo the colours of this old-fashioned water jug. The flowers are set in asymmetrical style, with a bold main line following the lip of the jug to the right.

CONTRASTING ARRANGEMENTS

The term contrast, in the art of flower arranging, refers not only to colour, but also to form, texture and the individual character of the material. This means that you could have a design in monochromatic colours combined with contrasting shapes and texture.

Obviously, contrast also refers to colour and how drab life would be without it. But never confuse contrast with discord of any kind. Two synonyms of this word are strife and harsh, neither of which has any place in the flower arranger's dictionary.

In fact, contrast presents a challenge: it is relatively quick and easy to make a small design with one kind of flower in one colour. But as soon as you begin to add other subjects, then you need to evaluate how much, where and, indeed, if. Decisions have to be made all along the line, entirely on your own for, as with colour, no two people will agree one hundred per cent on any given balance of contrast.

An arrangement of antirrhinums in two colours (*right*). Alone, the yellow or pink would be bland, but the longer yellow stems, spiced with a smaller quantity of pink flowers on shorter stems create an agreeable contrast of colour. Rust coloured chrysanthemums complete the design.

Opposite: The vertical design of arum lilies (*left*) is a little unimaginative in this whitemilk glass container, and the texture of the flowers is very similar to the finish of the vase. *Centre*: Add five stems of column stock and a contrast in colour, form and texture is immediately introduced. This may prove too strong a contrast for some tastes, so several heads of lilac are added at the heart of the arrangement, providing a third variation in colour value and texture. *Right*: Close-up of lily and column stock. *Below*: A basket full of contrasts — wild flowers, florsts' flowers and garden flowers. And if the chrysanthemum is regarded as a winter flower, the arrangement is also a contrast of seasons, spanning spring, early summer and winter.

GROUPING
COLOURS

Any material that has been grouped together becomes more significant than if it were scattered.

One of the main points in grouping colours is to know where to place certain colours to give the best effect in both the design and its location. Lighter colours can be used as highlights or focal interest.

while darker colours can be used to give depth, or to accentuate lighter colours. Most colours are usually more lively if they are not grouped too evenly throughout an arrangement. Think of the design as if you were painting it. 'Paint in' one group of material at a time, leaving one or two stems for the finishing touches.

This tall, circular black container (*below*) is a lovely base for the multi-coloured arrangement of liatris, yellow iris, red anemones and yellow broom (cytisus). Notice how the colours of the larger central flowers are echoed around the edges with lighter-weight blooms.

Grouping your colours. Here the main lines or purple are set in position (*above*). They form two distinct groups which are linked together with a single bloom.

The addition of broom and iris echoes and expands the lines of liatris. The iris — a particularly lovely variety called Angel's Wings — is lemon with white-tipped petals, which is less emphatic than plain yellow.

Parallel form (*below*). In this type of grouping the aim is to imitate nature by arranging the material such as it grows. Thus, the taller flowers remain on long stems, while shorter ones are placed exactly as they grow, giving an interesting balance of scale and proportion. The base is usually — as here — a shallow dish-like container, which is packed with foam and topped with fresh moss.

An all-yellow design is given a strong focal point by inserting a few stems of magenta stock into the centre (*above*).

MONOCHROMATIC
COLOURS

Mono means one, thus a monochromatic arrangement is a design of one colour only. First decide on the colour and then introduce all available tints and shades of the basic colour. Obviously, it is not possible to blend as an artist would mix paint on a palette, but flowers of the same hue and those which are lighter and darker than the chosen colour may be included.

They may be flowers of the same family, but they might also be varied, which would introduce a contrast in texture as well.

Monochromatic harmony is probably the most soothing of all colour

Purple liatris with paler coloured lilac are the main materials used in this monochromatic design. Liatris is used to establish the radiating lines, which are further emphasized by the rich deep purple tones of the foliage. The pale lilac on shorter stems is inserted at the base of the design.

combinations, for the eye and mind are not assailed by possibly conflicting tints. No two people see colour alike and what gives pleasure to one may not please another.

However, arrangements in mono-chromatic harmony – and here the word harmony is particularly appropriate – sug-gest peace and lack of conflict. Such arrangements are obviously very accept-able in hospitals or in any situation where a calm atmosphere should be preserved. The colour chosen should also be appro-priate to the situation. For example, to take a bouquet of red carnations to some-one who is ill in an attempt 'to cheer him up' will probably have the reverse effect, while deep pink or a soft clover colour might achieve success. Colour is a con-tinually absorbing aspect of flower arranging and every combination pres-ents both its problems and challenges.

Delphiniums are obvious flowers for monochromatic treatment as well as for perpendicular designs. They range from the palest blue to a really rich ultramarine, here underlined by the blue of the glass container. Foliage of contrasting shapes completes the arrangement.

FOLIAGE ARRANGEMENTS

Sometimes foliage is regarded as just a background material. It is, of course, indispensable both for masking the foam support and as a background for the flower arrangement. There are also several types of very distinctive foliage that can be designed without flowers, as mixed foliage arrangements in their own right. I remember a presentation given by an eminent Japanese designer living in Britain who used nothing but foliage in his designs, and yet none of the material was particularly rare. He created many delightful arrangements, some in the Japanese style and some in the Western style.

Foliage should, of course, be selected with as much care as flowers, keeping an eye on colour, shape and texture. There are leaves with a definite blue-grey tint, others with a yellow-cream bias, while some are grey or silver, to mention but a few. Most leaves condition well by being submerged for several hours in clear water. Examples that respond well to this technique are hosta, begonia rex and chlorophytum. Those leaves with a hairy or velvety texture should not be submerged, but should be stood in shallow water. Young leaves are quite charming, with their fresh green shapes, but unfortunately they do not last very long. Some, however, will enjoy being stood in a few inches of quite hot water, to which flower food has been added.

The enormous variety of flowers and foliage that blooms throughout the year, gives ample choice for planning a simple or elaborate arrangement, and for buying flowers to suit your budget.

A contrast in colour and shape, with the graceful feathery grevillea at the centre of this arrangement. A lovely dark red is introduced by the zebrina to the left, which makes an interesting contrast with the yellow/green variegation of peperomia on the right.

The material (*above*) chosen for a green arrangement is not strictly foliage alone since the seed heads of some bluebells have been included to vary texture.

Using these simple materials this arrangement (*right*) has been designed for all-round effect, with grasses forming a central line.

The delicately shaded green and cream vase with its slender neck is an obvious choice for a green arrangement. The bell-like flowers of the tolmiea make an interesting contrast with the deep red fingers of the hellebore leaves and the feathery, downward-curving hedge parsley.

Further contrast has been added at the centre of the design on the left with the addition of hellebore flowers and the still-green flowers of the *Viburnum opulus* or snowball tree.

A third alternative. The hellebore flowers and *Viburnum opulus* have gone, and the deep red of the hellebore foliage is given prominence once more. Below, new contrast is provided with the introduction of four types of variegated leaf.

SPRING
FLOWERS

Spring flowers offer the flower arranger a fantastic range of materials, including colour, form and size – a complete palette from which to choose, mix, match and harmonize.

In the Northern Hemisphere, the daffodil is the true spring flower and, even though it can often be bought in flower shops well before Christmas, it is still thought of as the signal that winter is almost past. It is also one of the earliest-known flowers. Gerard, the herbalist writes in his first *Herball* of 1599, that Theocritus speaks of a 'nymphs idyll', describing maidens gathering sweetly-scented wild daffodils and hyacinths (presumably the early bluebell).

Daffodils are probably one of the most popular of flowers, for they are produced commercially in huge quantities out of their natural season, which means that, in cool climates, they can be enjoyed from early December through to March. For many years now daffodils have been sold in fairly tight bud as it was found that the flowers suffered less damage if they were harvested and packed at what is called the 'gooseneck' stage. That is, when the flower has turned downwards ready to show colour. To cut them before this stage would be too early and the flowers would not develop to their true size and beauty. Tulips, irises and freesias are also commercially packed in bud, as are many hybrid lilies such as the lovely orange Enchantment, clear yellow Destiny or Connecticut King, and the beautiful white variety called Juliana. They obviously travel better in bud and will open gradually to give a succession of flowers all on one stem.

If spring flowers are bought fresh from the florist, their conditioning is very simple. As a general rule, all bulb-grown flowers should be stood in only a small amount of water, about 3-4in (8-10 cm), to which flower food has been added. It is not always essential to cut the stems of daffodils, tulips or freesias, as they drink easily, and cutting the stem-end would cause the flower to open more readily.

Anemones, also, prefer a shallow amount of water. Most lilies usually have rather woody stems and these should be cut with a sharp knife before being conditioned in shallow flower-food solution. It is advisable to leave your spring flowers for an hour or so in as cool and dark a place as possible so that the stems can take up plenty of water. This will reward you with healthy-looking blooms and several days' longer vase life.

Tulips like to curve towards the light and frequently this adds movement and interest to a design. But if you want your tulips to stand upright, you may have to insert wires into their stems, taking care not to puncture them. Insert the wire upwards until you feel it come into contact with the seedbox inside the tulip. The flower should then remain nice and stiff. Polyanthus, like daffodils and tulips, look their best when arranged comparatively informally. Unlike most other flowers, they seem to prefer to be packed tightly into the vase. This does not sound like flower arranging at all, but usually when they are used singly, they hang their heads no matter how well they have been conditioned. Garden-grown lilies-of-the-valley are very similar in this respect, preferring to be 'arranged' in a close-packed, handmade bouquet and set into a narrow vase, rather than each stem being put in separately. All flowers enjoy an overhead spray with clear water after being arranged.

Try, whenever possible to use each flower's natural foliage for arranging. Tulips have plenty of leaves, as do irises and violets. Polyanthus leaves will droop unless they have been submerged in water for at least an hour, but after a good 'drowning' they will last just as long as the flowers.

The many beautiful spring-flowering garden shrubs are excellent for large arrangements. Sprays of bright yellow forsythia, delicate prunus, very early-flowering winter jasmine and 'fingers' of witch-hazel on bare branches will all mix happily, either with bulb-grown flowers or by themselves.

Tolmiea

Gerbera

Alyssum

Lily

Lilac

Iris

Nettle (yellow archangel)

Carnation

Lily

An arrangement in yellow and white: daffodils, narcissus and nettles in a crystal goblet bring all the freshness of spring into the living room.

Broom

Anemone

Hellebore

Daffodil

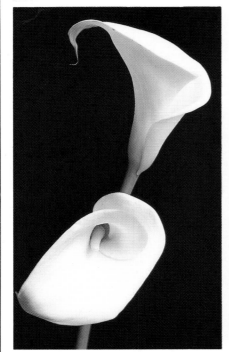

Arum lily

Liatris

Lily-of-the-valley

Japonica (Japanese quince)

Cowslip

Ixia

Anthurium

Freesia

SUMMER
FLOWERS

Summer brings an abundance of flowers in many varieties of size, shape and colour. Even if you do not have a garden, you can still plant flowers in window boxes, planters, and hanging baskets. As long as the plants have light, regular watering and feeding, they will reward you with as many blooms as they would in the garden.

It is a joy to be able to pick flowers from the garden, cutting them precisely when you want them and standing them in water before arranging them.

If there is a quantity of one sort, you can make a one-type flower arrangement with emphasis on line and shape. And if there are still too many, then they can be dried gradually for the winter months. If there are many different types of flowers all blooming at once you can mix them together, making sure that the smaller flowers are not overpowered by the larger varieties.

Before cutting the flowers, do remember to have a container with about 5in (13cm of water and flower food ready to put them in. In this way your flowers will last as long as possible. Summer storms can spoil lovely blooms, so sometimes it is better to bring them indoors rather than leave them to be beaten down by wind and rain.

Sedum

Philadelphus

Delphinium

Geranium

Antirrhinum

Molucella

Antirrhinum

Larkspur

Sunflower

Potato flower

Strelitzia

Double poppy

Eremurus

Phlox

Foxglove

Rhododendron

Marigold

Clarkia

Clematis

Candytuft

Cymbidium

Geranium

Single poppy

AUTUMN
FLOWERS

This is the season of mists and mellow fruitfulness, with string beans, blackberries and grapes – hanging thick and black patiently waiting to be made into wine; bright orange Chinese lanterns (physalis), multi-coloured statice and honesty 'moons', and the pinky-mauve fingers of autumn crocus (colchicum), which seem to shoot up when least expected. There are also Michaelmas daisies and dahlias. These are just some of the flowers that provide us with material for autumn arrangements.

The whole dahlia family offers a fantastic choice of colour, shape and size. It includes huge decorative blooms the size of a dinner plate, the medium-sized pompom variety, the spiky cactus type and the really tiny button dahlias which, incidentally, make perfect buttonholes, while the creamy white variety make ideal yet simple bridal bouquets. Even though dahlias, and many other flowers, are circular, a line effect can be achieved by carefully grading the colour and size. Try to use each flower the way it faces naturally and profit by any curving stem that will emphasize your line. Remove most of the foliage, for however much one enjoys leaves, dahlia foliage is not always very decorative and it does need a lot of water. Side buds should be cut off and inserted on their own stems. If left on the main stem, they will quickly droop.

Sedum

Erigeron

Gladiolus

Statice

Below: The warm golden colours of autumn are reflected in this asymmetrical arrangement of yellow cactus and orange and red pompom dahlias. The container, an unusual pottery jug, forms a perfect contrast to the rather busy texture of the flowers. The stems are set in soaked foam and the whole arrangement can be gently lifted out in order to add more water. This should be done frequently since dahlias are greedy drinkers.

Physalis

Cactus and pompom dahlias

WILD
FLOWERS

Many wild flowers although generally more delicate than garden varieties are undoubtedly worth picking and arranging. They will need careful conditioning, but before that they should be protected from the sun and wind as soon as they are collected. It is the sun and wind that absorb moisture from around the flowers.

So often one sees wild flowers and by the time they can be conditioned they are almost past redemption. It is a good idea to take with you a small knife and several plastic bags, even a jar or two with a little water, whenever possible. A large spray will also help to keep the flowers reasonably fresh until they can have a proper drink. Many wild flowers will respond well to being stood in quite hot water, while foliage and large stems should be submerged for up to 12 hours, after which time they will be quite strong and ready to be arranged.

Plan your wild flower designs in the same way as other garden flowers – picking only those you require. Do not over-pick and remember it is illegal to collect protected species.

A free arrangement of wood-sorrel, speedwells and buttercups in a clear glass jar (*above*). No need for foam here — the flowers are simply grouped and set in the jar to be held in place by its slender neck.

Bluebells (*left*), the delicate spring flowers of the woodlands, can bring a reminder of the countryside into your home.